It's Time to Eat a Pomegranate

Walter the Educator

Silent King Books
A WhichHead Entertainment Imprint

Copyright © 2024 by Walter the Educator

All rights reserved. No part of this book may be reproduced in any manner whatsoever without written per- mission except in the case of brief quotations embodied in critical articles and reviews.

First Printing, 2024

Disclaimer

This book is a literary work; the story is not about specific persons, locations, situations, and/or circumstances unless mentioned in a historical context. Any resemblance to real persons, locations, situations, and/or circumstances is coincidental. This book is for entertainment and informational purposes only. The author and publisher offer this information without warranties expressed or implied. No matter the grounds, neither the author nor the publisher will be accountable for any losses, injuries, or other damages caused by the reader's use of this book. The use of this book acknowledges an understanding and acceptance of this disclaimer.

IT'S TIME TO EAT A POMEGRANATE

It's Time to Eat a Pomegranate is a collectible early learning book by Walter the Educator suitable for all ages belonging to Walter the Educator's Time to Eat Book Series. Collect more books at WaltertheEducator.com

USE THE EXTRA SPACE TO TAKE NOTES AND DOCUMENT YOUR MEMORIES

POMEGRANATE

It's time to eat, let's gather 'round,

It's Time to Eat a
Pomegranate

A pomegranate treat is what I've found!

Red and round, like a shiny ball,

A special fruit for one and all!

From faraway lands where the sunshine's bright,

A pomegranate grows with all its might.

On the outside, smooth and red,

But inside, what's waiting to be fed?

Oh, pomegranate, jewel so bright,

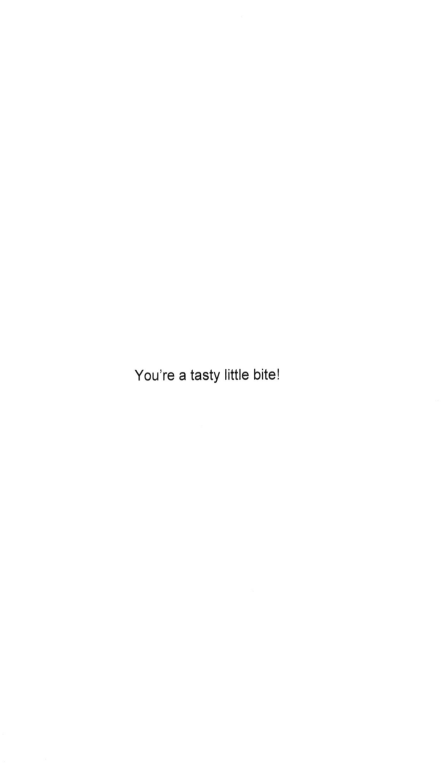
You're a tasty little bite!

Full of seeds, so fun to eat,

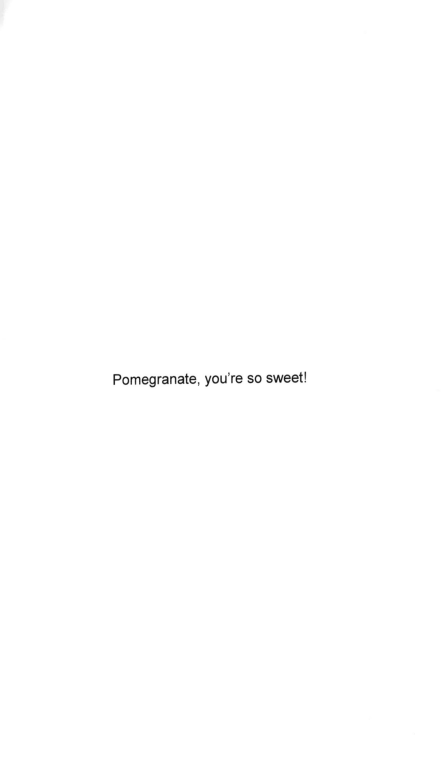

Pomegranate, you're so sweet!

I slice you open, and what do I see?

Tiny red jewels just waiting for me!

Each little seed, like a gem in my hand,

A treasure from the pomegranate land!

I pick one out, pop it in my mouth,

It's juicy and fresh, from the sunny south!

A burst of flavor, sweet and tart,

Pomegranate, you fill my heart!

Oh, pomegranate, jewel so bright,

It's Time to Eat a
Pomegranate

You're a tasty little bite!

Full of seeds, so fun to eat,

Pomegranate, you're so sweet!

You're fun to open, fun to share,

With all your seeds hidden everywhere!

A tiny bite in every bead,

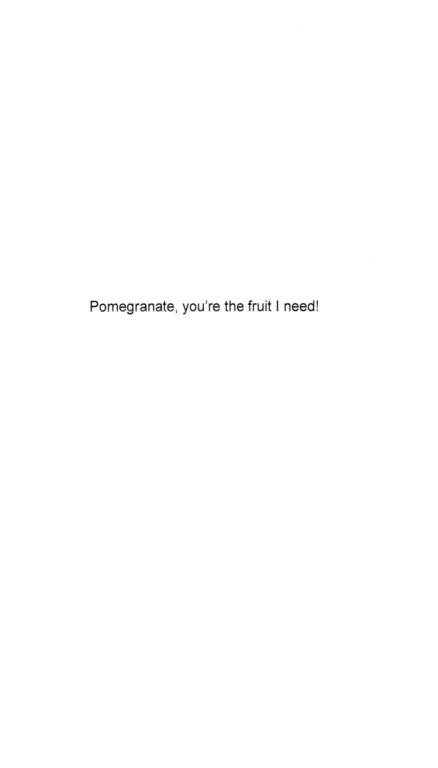
Pomegranate, you're the fruit I need!

Your seeds are crunchy, juicy too,

With every bite, I feel brand new!

It's Time to Eat a
Pomegranate

You help me grow, you make me strong,

A pomegranate snack all day long!

In salads, drinks, or just on a plate,

Pomegranate is always great!

In jams or sauces, you add delight,

A burst of flavor in every bite!

Oh, pomegranate, jewel so bright,

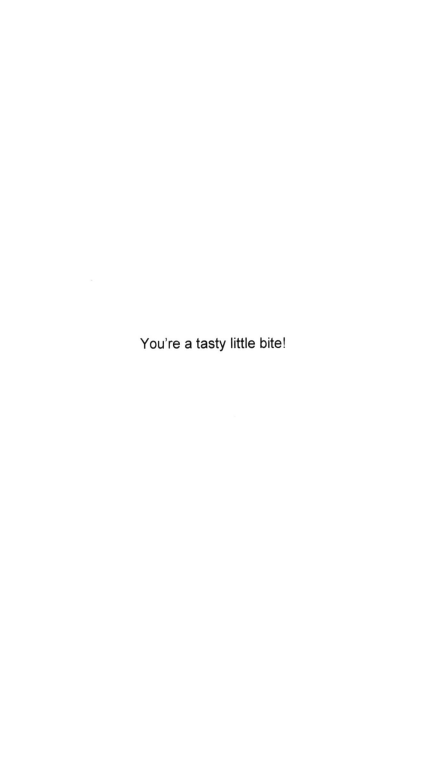

You're a tasty little bite!

Full of seeds, so fun to eat,

Pomegranate, you're so sweet!

ABOUT THE CREATOR

Walter the Educator is one of the pseudonyms for Walter Anderson. Formally educated in Chemistry, Business, and Education, he is an educator, an author, a diverse entrepreneur, and he is the son of a disabled war veteran. "Walter the Educator" shares his time between educating and creating. He holds interests and owns several creative projects that entertain, enlighten, enhance, and educate, hoping to inspire and motivate you. Follow, find new works, and stay up to date with Walter the Educator™ at WaltertheEducator.com

Milton Keynes UK
Ingram Content Group UK Ltd.
UKHW021938281024
450365UK00018B/1148

9 798330 491964